"Life Was Never Meant to Be a Struggle"

"Life Was Never Meant to Be a Struggle"

Stuart Wilde

Hay House, Inc.
Carlsbad, California • Sydney, Australia

Published and distributed in the United States by:

Hay House, Inc., P.O. Box 5100
Carlsbad, CA 92018-5100
(800) 654-5126

Book Design: Highpoint Graphics, Claremont, CA
Cover Design: Christy Salinas

Library of Congress Cataloging-in-Publication Data

Wilde, Stuart,
    Life was never meant to be a struggle. Stuart Wilde.
        p.   cm.
    ISBN 1-56170-535-7 (tradepaper)
    1. Spiritual life.   2. Struggle.   3. Relaxation.   I. Title
BL624.W545 1998
158--dc21   97-53042
        CIP

                    ISBN 1-56170-535-7

            04 03 02 01   13 12 11 10

    First Published in 1987 by Nacson & Sons, Pty.,
                    Sydney, Australia

    2nd printing, January 1995, by Hay House, Inc.
            10th printing, August 2001

                Printed in Canada

"Life was never meant to be a struggle, just a gentle progression from one point to another, much like walking through a valley on a sunny day."

— Stuart Wilde

CONTENTS ❧

CHAPTER ONE ✤

The Strugglers' Hall of Fame

Do you remember being told as a child that if you wanted to make it in life you would have to work hard? That life involves pain and struggle; that you'd have to earn love and acceptance; and that, if you wanted to come out on top, you'd have to put in an incredible effort? I certainly remember my mother saying to me, "Struggle ennobles the soul."

But who says this is true? Look at nature. It expends a certain effort in sustaining itself but it does *not* struggle. Does the tiger in the forest get up in the morning and say, "I'll struggle like crazy today and hopefully by suppertime I'll get something to eat"? No way. It just rises, has a little sniff under its tiger armpits or does whatever tigers do at breakfast time, and heads out. At noon, there on the path is lunch, provided courtesy of the Great Spirit. Okay, the last 30 yards involves the tiger in a bit of rushing about. But that can hardly be construed as struggle.

You, too, may have to cross town to pick up a check. But there is a great difference between struggle and effort. Our physical condition as humans involves effort, but struggle is effort laced with emotion and desperation.

Think of this: If you accept full responsibility for your life, you will accept that your destiny is created by you. And that your life is basically a symbol of your inner-most thoughts and feelings—of what you believe about yourself.

Now if, over a period of years, you've laid down several hundred thousand thoughts in your subconscious that say, "Life is a struggle," naturally you would project that from your inner feelings. Even if you weren't consciously aware of that aspect of your inner self, the thought would still lie deep within you and show up constantly in your life.

Whenever a project starts to flow too well, or things become too easy, your inner self emits an energy that says, "Warning! Warning! This is too simple. Let us self-destruct this project or relationship and come at it the hard way, so we can experience circumstances that are congruent with our inner belief that life is a struggle."

So things fall apart, and you feel like you're trying to push a peanut up Everest with your nose. Eventually, once you've suffered the slings and arrows of outrageous fortune for a while, the inner self pulls you to a watered-down version of circumstances that would have been yours anyway weeks ago and without effort.

This booklet helps you identify struggle, discover the reasons for it, and *eliminate* it. But first let us look at some of the characters in the Strugglers' Hall of Fame. I'm sure you'll have fun recognizing them from among your friends and acquaintances.

The Hero: Men like struggling, but then so do some women. The male version goes something like this: "If I bust a gut and hurtle around trying hard, people will see me as a good man and treat me with respect. Whether I get results or not matters little, as long as I am seen to be making a valiant effort. To make sure everyone acknowledges my heroism, I'll create an entire theater of frantic action, hectic schedules, meetings of earth-shattering importance, long hours, and constant pressure. Of course, this pantomime will make me a bit tense. But that is all part of the act, for the tension will be seen by others as my taking responsibility, and they will love and respect me for that. Won't they?"

If the truth be known, the answer is "no." In fact, anyone with perception will see this male as a complete idiot. His weakness, namely a lack of personal acceptance, stands out a mile. He has chosen sacrifice as his fate, in the hope of winning affection or acknowledgment. His frantic actions only serve to underline that he is out of control and hasn't a *clue* about what he is doing.

Another common struggler is **The Terrorist.** Because this fellow is uncomfortable with himself, he finds he can't deal with society. He was either born disadvantaged, has never been accepted, or he bears some other kind of grudge. He therefore has to operate outside of society and finds it hard to accept help from anyone. He struggles through a hundred and one projects that never quite come off. Even if he does make a success of a relationship or project, it seems to him a hollow victory—what he wants is acceptance, not success. So he'll usually self-destruct his successes, then move on to struggle at something else.

If the terrorist ever finds himself within the mainstream—if he gets a job in a corporation, for example—he'll find fault with that situation. He'll sneer at it and attempt to change or destroy it. Usually, his actions will threaten those around him—and sooner or later he'll be tossed out.

Because the terrorist has to *fight* the system rather than use it, he never gets what he wants. No one supports him. If he *does* find someone who loves and accepts him, he disregards that support, focusing instead on all those aspects of nonrecognition that are a part of his life.

The third type of struggler is the **Professional Wimp.** This person is so weak, so lacking in the ability to command life, that he allows everyone to lead him around by the nose. It makes him angry, and he will protest his rights from a position that he feels is logical and just. But his struggle results from weak energy. He gets nowhere and no one cares.

There is a variation on this theme: the **"Spiritual" Wimp.** This character has a huge ego and feels that God dropped him off on earth so he could sit around being "special." He is usually so "holy" that he can't soil his hands with life. He expects people to treat him like a god and to honor him anyway. Usually he struggles like crazy, for people find it hard to accept his lifestyle, and his failure threatens them.

One of the common female archetypes, **The Goddess,** is similar to the male. She plays a game called, "Please accept me, for I am great. I am really a goddess, and I am as strong as any male—or stronger." To act out her pantomime, she dresses in male clothes, drives fast cars, and gets superaggressive (to make up for her lack of confidence). And she, too, hurtles out and plays the achiever's game of her male counterpart.

In truth, being a goddess is hard work; you constantly have to sustain a celestial pose. Usually, others won't see you as a goddess, so you expend energy in the hope of convincing them. By trying to emulate the male, the female is actually saying, "I know I am weaker." This, of course, is not true. Most women are spiritually stronger than males, if only they would realize it.

Another female character has a play called **"Wilting Wallflower."** It goes like this: "I am just a helpless little person. I am weak

and don't understand life. I can't add fig-
ures or mend a fuse; my emotions are all
over the parking lot. Please save me, please
look after me. That way I can sit someplace
and not do much of anything."

This works to a certain extent, for sooner or later the "lifesaver" type shows up to
assist her. The problem is that the lifesaver,
be they male or another female, will only
save the Wallflower once or twice. Then
they move on because there's nothing in it
for them.

As the Wilting Wallflower plays out her
act, it gets harder and harder for her to feel
any self-worth. Sooner or later that lack of
self-worth pulls her to people who will
delight in manipulating her. Her spiral of
struggle is self-perpetuating for, in order to
get the attention she craves, she has to
create more and more dramatic scenarios
of helplessness. Eventually she drifts into
playing victim.

You all know the type. When you meet her, she pours out a litany of disasters. There is nothing you can do for her because she's not asking for help, she just wants you to commiserate. Quite often you will want to punch her in the nose just to keep her happy.

What do these characters have in common? First, they are all pretty stupid. They are playing out those facets of their personalities that are not truth. Yet, with just a small adjustment in attitude, they could move from struggle into flow.

You have to work hard at creating struggle, whereas flow is a natural condition. It comes from accepting yourself and watching your life so that it's reasonably balanced most of the time.

ᔐ ᔐ ᔐ

CHAPTER TWO ∽

Identifying Struggle

*B*ecause struggle is a programmed response and is natural to many, we often find ourselves struggling without realizing we're doing so. The first step in reducing struggle in your life is to identify it.

If you've read my book *Affirmations,* you may remember that I suggested that you take time to go into every aspect of your life, and evaluate what you get out of it in relation to what you put in. I asked you to plug in the "struggle-o-meter"—a mythical device created by your mind to gauge the levels of struggle you exert.

The main areas you review are:

1) your physical body

2) your emotional balance

3) your relationships

4) your physical living circumstances

5) your finances

6) your attitude to the world around you

7) your ability to handle conflict

8) your ability to handle stress

9) your psychological state

10) your spiritual balance

1. Your Physical Body

If your body is weak, it is either a genetic

problem or an imbalance you created. If your weakness is genetic, you can change a "poor me" attitude to one of strength by realizing that your weakness is a gift. It allows you to express power in spite of your condition. It's like having one or two oarsmen in your boat and no oar for them. So what? The boat can make it anyway. A bit slower perhaps, but it will get there. And the extra time it takes will allow you to enjoy the journey more fully.

If your weakness is not genetic, fix it. Or at least express the most energy you can toward healing your body so that it doesn't dominate your life. As you put real effort into the healing, the rise in energy that results inspires you to go further. You will become happier and more balanced.

2. Your Emotional Balance

Emotional turmoil is yet another pro-grammed response. As children, we are taught to cry out to get what we want—and sometimes we carry that over into adult life. "If I create enough fuss, will you love me?"

Your reaction to an emotional situation is just your opinion; it is not necessarily truth. In any given situation, you can react dispassionately or otherwise, as you wish. Train yourself to be more forgiving of yourself, more detached, and you will see your life in an infinite sense—not a finite sense. Everything becomes a lesson, a way of strengthening you.

Gauge the level of your emotional rage. Everyone has it. If it comes up within you, do something positive to release it at once. Communication usually works.

Also, avoid conflict. Remember—only the fool stands and fights; the sage walks away. It's pointless to get your knickers in a twist if a certain person fails to react the way you want. It's best to avoid people and situations that drive you crazy. Remember

to vote with your feet. If a situation is
untenable or unchangeable, walk away.

3. Your Relationships

Through relationships we learn about
ourselves, because people around us reflect
back to us what we are. That is why many
relationships are hard. If your relationships
cause you to struggle, ask yourself why.
What opinion do you hold about the relationship or yourself that prevents it from
going the way you want? What are you trying to push against? What is your level of
giving and receiving? Are you allowing
yourself to be ripped off, and, if you are, is
that okay, or do you want to change that?

4. Your Living Circumstances

Are your circumstances designed to
nurture you? Do they support you? Or are
you at the mercy of circumstances? If so,
what are you going to do about it? What is

the level of struggle here? For example, does the home you live in take so much effort to maintain that you get out of it less than you put in?

5. *Your Finances*

The question here is not, "Do you have enough money?" Rather, it is, "Is your life contained and balanced within the money you *do* have?" If it's not, you'll usually find yourself struggling to maintain a lifestyle that your ego/personality feels it needs, but which your current energy may not be able to sustain.

6. *Your Attitude to the World Around You*

Your life—your evolution—is your business; what others do is their business. If you let the world affect how you feel, what you are saying is, "I do not make my own decisions, I just have a Pavlovian response to anything that may twang my emotions."

Are you struggling to fix the world? If so, why? It's a bit of an ego trip when people think they can fix things. If you can see the world as an infinite evolution—the way God would see it—you would know that it's more or less perfect and does not need fixing. It's only when we view the world within the finite context of our emotions and ego that it looks less than perfect.

You can instantly become happy and free by deciding to leave the world alone and concentrate instead on yourself. By strengthening yourself, you serve all humanity. Each of us is linked to one another.

7. Your Ability to Handle Conflict

Conflict is always just a divergence of opinions. Are you struggling to convince others that your opinion is right? And if you are right, so what? To win a moral victory at the expense of your sanity is dumb.

8. *Your Ability to Handle Stress*

In a crowded world, with all the obliga-tions we take on, stress is natural. Do you react emotionally or unemotionally to stress? Do you understand how to handle it? Some top-notch strugglers like to create stress so they can feel excitement in their lives. They live on their adrenals. You don't have to go bananas in order to have fun or to feel exhilarated about life.

9. *Your Psychological State*

If your psychological state causes you anguish, it will be either a by-product of your physical state or, once more, of your opinion. How much of each applies to you?

10. *Your Spiritual Balance*

Balance is natural. Whenever you force something to happen, you have to come off-balance to do so. How much do you exist in the flow? And how much do you have to push?

The difference between a spiritual person and a person who is less evolved is that spiritual persons are *real*. They live within the truth of the inner self, what many call the Higher Self. They don't play games; they don't have to make excuses. They can say with conviction, "I am what I am." They realize that they are neither all-knowing nor perfect and are happy with that.

Because people are generally weak, they tend to be phony and play out a character who is not them—who is not truth. So they struggle to maintain a Jekyll and Hyde existence. One is the official image the ego/personality says has to be maintained, and the other, what they really are. Often, people are so settled in their ego's reality that they won't realize what the Higher Self within is telling them. They see the fake character as real and will struggle to maintain that. Their energies

and lifestyle become so fragmented that
every effort to achieve anything becomes a
painful grind.

↬ ↬ ↬

CHAPTER THREE ∽

The Strugglers' Hit Parade

*B*elow, I've listed eleven of the most common reasons or aspects of struggle—the Strugglers' Hit Parade. Do any of these apply to you? If so, let's look at that. In the next section, I'll give you a powerful action plan to go beyond this.

Strugglers Crave Acceptance

Most strugglers have low self-esteem. This causes them to constantly seek the acceptance and approval of others. Yet the acknowledgment they seek is rarely forth-coming, and usually doesn't satisfy them even when they get it. This causes frustra-tion. Because they lack a sense of identity, a sense of knowing or accepting who they really are, they shift their attention from what is real—inside themselves—to the symbols of life, which are not real—outside themselves. They see the *things* around them as confirmation that they are okay, rather than confirming who they are with-in themselves.

Thus, life for them is a struggle to sus-tain a status that is fake. And no amount of baubles or bangles will keep this struggler happy, for acquisitions have only short emotional shelf lives. If strugglers buy, say, a new yacht, they can say, "Please accept me because I own this yacht." They are excited for a while as they play out the theater of yachting. But sooner or later, the emotional pleasure of the yacht drains away, and they then have to go and find something else to fill their acceptance needs.

If, by chance, life does not go the way the struggler wants, they get mad and frustrated—because now they are detached from their confirming symbols. They not only feel worthless, but they don't have the confirmation they constantly crave.

Strugglers Often Have Big Egos

Strugglers usually have big egos because they allow their egos/personalities to talk them into a greater opinion of themselves than they can sustain. It has to be exaggerated because they don't believe, or see, worth in what they are. So naturally, to compensate, they exaggerate life in the hope that at least some of it will come off.

You are divine spirit within a body, and you are finite ego/personality. The divine spirit or Higher Self knows the direction in which it is headed and has most of the power—the inner power. The ego holds the outer power. When your ego/personality is going in the same direction as the Higher Self, things flow. But if the ego/personality is off in another direction, struggle ensues. Remember, spirituality is being real, living in truth. The ego/personality lives in a variation of the truth, which is its opinion.

Strugglers Feel That Struggle Is Noble

To justify the fact that their lives are out of control, strugglers like to feel that struggle is noble—that somehow God is pleased with them for struggling. If you were God, you would fall over laughing at that one.

Strugglers Set Unrealistic Goals

The ego/personality decides what it needs to keep itself happy, and it decides

how fast it wants those circumstances to
come about. Often the struggler will set
goals that are unrealistic. They may decide
on a level, and say to themselves, "I will
have that in six months." But their energy
is not there yet on a metaphysical level. So
there is a variance between what they
believe is possible and what is *actually* possible. Usually the struggler will be impa-
tient and push like crazy to make the dead-
lines they've set.

In that headlong plunge for the goal,
strugglers gather a metaphysical wake
around themselves, similar to the wake of
a ship. That wake is hard to operate with,
for their lives will lack fluidity. The wake
creates an energy that is impossible for the
Higher Self to penetrate.

They will be heading north, say, and the
Higher Self will be whispering, "South,
south," but the struggler does not hear it.
The struggler sees only the goal, not the

path. They're trapped by their opinion of how to reach the goal. No other possibilities exist. So life moves out of their way, leaving them to operate in a barren land. The strugglers are forced to head in the direction they've set for themselves.

Often, in the frantic effort to make the goal, they miss the side-turning that would offer simplicity or a shortcut. This kind ploughs on regardless of pain and anguish, or of whether their actions are appropriate or effective.

Strugglers Lack Understanding

Strugglers lack understanding. Sometimes it is just a lack of knowing about the physical plane and how the marketplace works. Usually the strugglers will have dropped out sometime back and be drifting, for they are not really prepared to concentrate on life and learn how the world works. They usually can't be bothered—struggle is easier.

It's common for this type to feel that
the world owes them a living, and they get
upset when circumstances do not agree
with that point of view.

They also lack metaphysical knowledge.
They don't see how the Universal Laws
operate in their lives. So, rather than create
an energy and let life come to them, gradually and in its own time, they go after
life—and push it away through their needs
and emotion.

Strugglers Worry What Others Think

Strugglers are often very social animals.
They believe in a social reality, and they
accept the opinions of others as truth. This
forces them to live up to what are often the
unreal expectations of others. They worry
about what others think of them because
they are not sure of themselves.

To go past this trap, all you have to do is
to realize that your evolution through life is

sacrosanct. You are the only one who can decide what is best for you. Only you have the answers. What society thinks of you is totally irrelevant, for others do not have all the facts. Remember, people will always try to manipulate you into their way of thinking. They will want you to act in a way that supports them. When you no longer feel the need to win their approval—because basically you have won your own approval—their manipulations of you become meaningless.

As with little children, you can love them for the games they play, but you do not have to take part. You can walk away. In the end, the only true path for you is as an independent. It's only a matter of habit and the way you learn to react. By detaching you become free.

Strugglers Lack Stability

Stability is the key to a worry-free existence. This means balance in every area of

your life. This topic is dealt with extensive-
ly in my book *The Force*, but let us encap-
sulate the main point, which is:

To have balance and stability, you have to
exercise control over every area of your life.
This may not be possible as yet, but you can
move toward total self-realization bit by bit.
This means you are not going to let life tow
you around. You will develop the power to
say "no" to situations that are not a part of
your overall intention for yourself. You are
the general of your army, making choices
that constantly move you forward, toward
that higher energy you seek.

It also means that you have the right to
be satisfied with what you have and with
what you are right now. Otherwise, you'll
never reach a point where you are satisfied.
You have to be happy with your lot right
now. Just because your ego/personality
may have sold you on an alternative pro-
gram, it doesn't mean that you can't settle

within the one you have now. There must
be lessons to learn here and now. If those
lessons are not learned, if you do not
accept what you have created for yourself,
your energy does not move forward. By
resisting, by not adapting to change, you
stagnate. Some professional strugglers love
to bang their heads against the wall—it
feels so good when they stop.

Today is part of your life's curriculum.
Learn it and tomorrow will look after itself.
Think of this: If you've made it through
life so far with what you know, it's obvious
that you will make it through the rest of
your life once you possess greater knowledge and objectivity. That is truth.

Strugglers Often Lack Concentration

Concentration is a key discipline in personal growth and development. Everything else is meaningless, for your power
rests where your consciousness flows.

When you are centered and concentrating on what you are doing, you not only derive more from your actions, but all your power—inner and outer—is being used to empower your actions.

The mind hates to concentrate. Most people cannot center on one idea for more than a minute. Now if you train the laser light of your intention in a direction, you empower that direction with your energy. If 15 seconds later you are distracted by a thought—"Did I leave the iron on?"—your power has gone.

By developing a goal, concentrating on it for a few seconds, and then becoming distracted—*and* by concentrating at various levels of intensity—you put into Universal Law such a hesitant, staccato message that it doesn't know what the hell you want.

Successful people set up a plan of action and concentrate on it until it's completed. Then they set up another. While working on an idea, they give it their full attention, empowering it with their consciousness until it becomes a reality.

Watch how your mind plays games with you. Often we start a project, and 15 minutes later the mind goes, "I hate having to concentrate on this. Let's have a cup of coffee." And so the project is put to one side. Or perhaps the phone rings; the caller has no idea what you are doing; their intention is expressed out of their need to speak to you. We allow the mind to use the telephone call to distract us rather than saying to the caller, "Thanks for calling, but I can't talk to you now; call back at Christmas." Through concentration you become powerful. Force your mind to concentrate, and you have won a battle over struggle.

Strugglers Have Poorly Designed Lifestyles

You are the general. Plot your battle plan and stay centered on it, but let the winds and currents of life allow you to flow to other areas. Designing your life is a matter of discipline. You need certain things, and you deserve them. But how do you get them with minimum effort? By cutting out those things that are superfluous. Toss the extra baggage out, and hold on to a life of simplicity. Constantly evaluate circumstances to see if things are worth the effort. Often you will find they are not.

Strugglers Lack Order

To go beyond struggle you have to have order. Otherwise you dissipate energy, wasting time in confusion.

Strugglers Lack Concerted Action in the Marketplace

You are a consciousness, a spirit, but you are also a physical being. There is a point when you will have to take your creativity to the people and sell it. That involves concerted action in the marketplace. Strugglers don't like concerted action. Yet through it, you get what you want.

෴ ෴ ෴

CHAPTER FOUR ∽

Dumping Struggle

There is no greater gift to yourself and to those around you than your deciding to dump struggle, for struggle is an unholy battle that you fight with yourself. It is not natural. Here are eight pointers you may wish to consider as you move from toil and struggle into absolute freedom.

Opinion

That which is struggle to one person is just gentle effort to another. Struggle is always how you feel about something—

your opinion. It is laced with negative
emotion. To dump struggle, you should
get used to asking yourself in each circum-
stance, "What is my underlying emotion
or opinion here?"

Perhaps your circumstances are not really a struggle, and all you have to do is make
a few slight changes in the way you view
things. Usually the correction can be made
simply and easily.

Timing

If things don't flow, ask yourself, "Am I
going too fast? Or am I too slow? Is this the
right time?" A great idea may result in a
total flop if presented at the wrong time.
Usually, things take longer than we expect
them to. This is because we can think faster
than we can act. So ideas have to have time
to incubate and come together, especially
when you need others to help you materialize your dreams. They need time to become

comfortable with your idea and to make it
their own, to move through whatever
considerations or opinions they may have.

Sometimes you may be moving too
slowly. This may be through a lack of
resolve or laziness or just plain dithering.
To make life work you have to face it full-
frontal—head out with a good plan and
trust in the Great Spirit to deliver. But
head out toward your goal even if it seems
a long way off. Nothing will carry you.
You will usually have to carry yourself.

Moving gracefully toward your goal,
you enjoy the journey and watch constantly to see if your actions are in keeping with
whatever energy you need to consummate
your desire.

Cast of Characters

At this time, the world has over five bil-
lion inhabitants. They are the characters
you will invite to be in your army of

helpers. Most will not be suitable, and many others will be busy in campaigns of their own.

But some are eminently suitable. To go beyond struggle, first you have to be able to accept the help of others, and, second, you have to choose your characters carefully. If you find yourself in a campaign with the cast already set, you must become a crafty general. You must get the most out of your people—given the circumstances, the goals, and what the budget allows.

It is a mathematical certainty that you will eventually eliminate most of the people who come into your life. We tend to think that the characters we have around us are the *only* characters. Not so.

I used to think that if I didn't get on with the kids in the neighborhood I would have no friends. So I adapted to what I felt they wanted of me. Truth is that there are billions of kids all over the place—but coming from my finite view as a small boy, I did not see that.

Never be afraid to let people go if they are not right; often that is the only way you can make room for the right person. Also, you are doing them a service. If they are square pegs in round holes, they need your help to move on to a more comfortable setting.

Is the Army Marching Without Boots?

To successfully materialize a battle plan, you have to go into the nitty-gritty. Do you have the wherewithal, the components you need? Or are you signing yourself up for a glorious disaster? Remember, just because you have a good idea, that is absolutely no reason to embark on it. Just because you love someone is no reason to marry them.

Let's say you want to open a shop. Do you have the capital? What do you know about shopkeeping? Is there a market for the products you want to sell? It's amazing how many people open businesses without ever finding out if there is really any demand for that business. They feel that because they really like pink shirts with little dots, everyone else in town will. Not so.

A good general does not commit his troops until he knows what he is getting into. For example, if you want to start a magazine in the USA, it takes about half-a-million dollars and five years to make it a financial success. Most new publications fold because the creators just don't know that simple fact.

Ask yourself prior to committing to anything, "Do I have the wherewithal to pull it off, and do I know what I am getting into?"

Am I Trying to Capture a Castle I Don't Really Need or Want?

What is your motivation for taking action? What is the level of your commitment? And do you actually want the end result, or are you going for something else instead? For example, are you dating the brother so you can be near the man you actually love? Is it worth the effort—or is there a simpler way?

In *Warriors in the Mist*, the five-day intensive seminar I used to put on in Taos, New Mexico, there's a section called "The Quickening." You learn to speed up your etheric energy and to evaluate your every move. You do this in light of the speed at which things materialize in your life.

Expending energy in a wasteful way is the road to poverty and struggle. You get bogged down in your own inefficiency. Eventually your life becomes an affirmation of helplessness. Remember, most of the paths you will be offered are totally inappropriate for you. At every turn, give yourself five good reasons for saying "no." And while walking into a relationship or project, look for the exit!

Am I Resisting?

To go beyond struggle, you have to go beyond rigid opinion. That means opening yourself up to change. Look to see how many paths there are available to you that you can easily identify. And look at how many possibilities you may have missed.

A young businesswoman came to see me recently. Over lunch she explained a business deal she was considering. Maneuvering the salt and pepper shakers across the table, she showed me how the deal would net her $100,000. She wanted to know what I felt about the plan.

As we talked, the waiter brought a finger bowl to our table and placed it haphazardly between the salt and pepper shakers. Suddenly, I saw that if the deal were divided into two parts it would change dramatically.

I asked if this was a possibility.

"Yes," she replied.

In analyzing the situation, we discovered that, expressed in its divided form, the deal would net her $480,000. She went away with her battle plan. The event reminded me that there is always more than one way to skin a rabbit.

Look at your options. Then play the devil's advocate and look for all the angles you may have missed.

If you find yourself in an uphill situation, ask yourself, "What am I resisting? What is it in this situation that I have missed and that is causing me turmoil?"

Am I Content with Conditions?

It always amazes me that people will put up with difficult conditions and actually like them. If conditions do not suit you, then set about changing them.

Am I in Control?

What is the level of control you exert? Are you rushing around like crazy? Have you relinquished control to others? If so, why? Was it because you felt powerless? Perhaps it felt comfortable to allow someone else to drive the bus? Why?

By exercising control, you command and become responsible. You also have the ability to alter things to suit yourself. And you're not prone to the whims of others.

Remember, it's okay to get what you want from life.

∽ ∽ ∽

CHAPTER FIVE ∽

Conclusion

*T*he very nature of our existence on the earth plane involves us in a certain amount of restriction. That is one of the lessons you come here to learn. Once that lesson is learned, you can move from restriction into absolute freedom, because ultimately your spiritual heritage is to be independent and free.

Effort is a part of our condition as physical beings, for we have to translate thoughts and feelings into physical action.

Struggle, however, is not natural. It is an unholy battle we fight with ourselves. But because it is a by-product of our personal imbalances, it's a condition we can easily go beyond.

By having the courage to identify and face the causes of struggle in your life, you grant yourself the power to transcend. Once you accept that *you* are the cause of struggle, you can then affirm, with certainty, that all struggle in your life can be eliminated, given time.

Further, because struggle is a programmed response—meaning that everyone is taught to struggle from an early age—it may take time to reprogram your attitudes for a more carefree existence. But it's fun to see yourself move gradually from various forms of anguish into celestial acceptance of yourself and the world around you.

To be free is a great gift. To achieve that, you do not need great amounts of money or influence or power. All you need is the ability to place yourself in a nonconfrontive mode. First, with yourself, and second, with the world around you.

As struggle begins to melt in the light of your balance and positivity, the new energy brings a freshness to your life, allowing your emotions to take on a resonating inner calm.

Inner calm allows you to pull more and more opportunities to yourself, because energy seeks its own kind. Balance and great good fortune can only come to a person who is balanced and feels fortunate.

Each day, from this moment on, toss out one aspect of your life that causes you difficulty. Make a note of your progress. See yourself moving inexorably toward your final goal—total freedom, exquisite happiness, absolute calm.

Once you reach that point and are able to sustain it for a while, teach it to others. Teach them that life was never meant to be a struggle.

They will thank you, for you will have set them free.

ᔕ ᔕ ᔕ

About the Author

Author and lecturer Stuart Wilde is one of the real characters of the self-help, human potential movement. His style is humorous, controversial, poignant, and transformational. He has written 14 books, including the very successful *Taos Quintet*, which includes: *Miracles, Affirmations, The Force, The Quickening*, and *The Trick to Money Is Having Some*. His books have been translated into 12 languages.

STUART WILDE
International Tour and
Seminar Information:

For information on Stuart Wilde's latest tour and seminar dates in the USA and Canada, contact:

White Dove International
P.O. Box 1000
Taos, NM 87571
(505) 758-0500 — phone
(505) 758-2265 — fax

Stuart's Website:
stuartwilde.com

～

We hope you enjoyed this Hay House
book. If you would like to receive a
free catalog featuring additional
Hay House books and products, or if
you would like information about the
Hay Foundation, please contact:

Hay House, Inc.
P.O. Box 5100
Carlsbad, CA 92018-5100
(760) 431-7695 or **(800) 654-5126**
(760) 431-6948 (fax) or
(800) 650-5115 (fax)

～

Please visit the Hay House Website at:
hayhouse.com